Celebrating American Holidays

HALLOWEEN

Kaite Goldsworthy

www.av2books.com

AV² provides enriched content that supplements and complements this book. Weigl's AV² books strive to create inspired learning and engage young minds in a total learning experience.

Your AV² Media Enhanced books come alive with...

Audio
Listen to sections of the book read aloud.

Video
Watch informative video clips.

Embedded Weblinks
Gain additional information for research.

Try This!
Complete activities and hands-on experiments.

Key Words
Study vocabulary, and complete a matching word activity.

Quizzes
Test your knowledge.

Slide Show
View images and captions, and prepare a presentation.

... and much, much more!

Go to www.av2books.com, and enter this book's unique code.

BOOK CODE

C829928

AV² by Weigl brings you media enhanced books that support active learning.

Published by AV² by Weigl
350 5th Avenue, 59th Floor
New York, NY 10118
Website: www.av2books.com   www.weigl.com

Copyright ©2012 AV² by Weigl
All rights reserved. No part of this publication may be reproduced, stored in a retrieval system, or transmitted in any form or by any means, electronic, mechanical, photocopying, recording, or otherwise, without the prior written permission of the publisher.

Library of Congress Cataloging-in-Publication Data

Goldsworthy, Kaite.
 Halloween / Kaite Goldsworthy.
  p. cm. -- (Celebrating American holidays. Arts & crafts)
 Includes index.
 ISBN 978-1-61690-681-8 (hardcover : alk. paper) -- ISBN 978-1-61690-687-0 (softcover : alk. paper)
 1. Halloween--Juvenile literature. 2. Halloween decorations--Juvenile literature. I. Title.
 GT4965.G65 2012
 394.2646--dc22
                      2011002423

Printed in the United States of America in North Mankato, Minnesota
1 2 3 4 5 6 7 8 9 0 15 14 13 12 11

062011
WE180511

Project Coordinator Jordan McGill   Art Director Terry Paulhus

Every reasonable effort has been made to trace ownership and to obtain permission to reprint copyright material. The publishers would be pleased to have any errors or omissions brought to their attention so that they may be corrected in subsequent printings.

Weigl acknowledges Getty Images as its primary image supplier for this title. Craft photos by Madison Helton.

CONTENTS

AV² Code 2

What is Halloween? 4

History of Halloween 6

The Celtic People of Ireland 8

Celebrating Today 10

Jack O'Lantern 12

Black Cats 14

Bats 16

Ghost of John 18

Halloween Foods 20

What Have You Learned? 22

Glossary/Index 23

Log on to www.av2books.com 24

What is Halloween?

On October 31 every year, the streets fill with children dressed in costumes. They go from door to door asking people for treats. Sometimes, they play tricks on people. This is Halloween, a holiday known for its ghosts and goblins.

Countries around the globe celebrate their own version of Halloween. While some celebrations are only on October 31, many other countries also celebrate the two days after. In South America and Mexico, celebrations start on October 31 and continue until November 2. Halloween is most popular in the United States and Canada, where celebrations include costume parties, trick-or-treating, and carving pumpkins.

History of Halloween

Halloween began as a **Celtic** festival. The end of October is a special time for Celtic people. Samhain is the Celtic New Year's Eve. Since the 5th century BC, Samhain, or "end of summer," has been celebrated on this date. Many Halloween **traditions** and symbols, such as bats and black cats, come from this festival. Dressing in costumes on Halloween began with Samhain.

Around the 7th century AD, the Catholic Church began celebrating some of its holy days at the same time of the year as Samhain. November 1st became known as "All Saints Day" or "All Hollows Day." The evening before, October 31, became known as "All Hallows Eve." Over time, this became "Halloween."

Create a Samhain Mask

During Samhain, people dressed in masks and costumes. This activity lets you create your own Samhain mask.

What You Need

- paper plate
- pencil
- markers
- string or ribbon
- scissors
- hole punch
- wool or yarn
- decorations of your choice

7 Easy Steps to Complete Your Mask

1. Cut your paper plate in half. Save one half.

2. Cut holes for your eyes. Be sure they are big enough for you to see properly.

3. Punch a hole in either side of your mask.

4. Decorate your mask using markers. Wool or yarn can be used for eyebrows or hair.

5. The leftover half of the paper plate can be used to cut out ears, a nose, or even a tongue.

6. If you wish, you can add other decorations of your choice for your own personal touch.

7. Tie the string or ribbon to each side. Slide the mask over your head, and show it to friends and family.

The Celtic People of Ireland

Between 1845 and 1849, the country of Ireland was plagued by the Great **Famine**. Diseased potato crops caused a serious food shortage. More than 1 million people died of starvation and disease. By 1851, almost 2 million Irish citizens had been forced to leave their homeland in order to escape the famine. Many moved to the United States and Canada, bringing their Celtic traditions with them. This included the holiday of Halloween.

One of the most common Halloween activities today, trick or treating, came from Irish tradition. November 2nd was "All Soul's Day" in the Catholic Church. On the eve of All Soul's Day, the poor would go from house to house asking for food in return for prayers for relatives who had passed away. Pastries called "soul cakes" would be handed out in exchange for these prayers.

A Ghostly Bag

Use this bag to hold all of your treats!

What You Need

- blank canvas tote bag
- paints in Halloween colors
- paintbrush
- paper plates
- scissors
- wiggle eyes
- felt, glitter, buttons, etc.
- fabric glue
- newspaper

8 Easy Steps to Complete Your Trick-or-Treat Bag

1 Lay newspaper over your work area. Put the canvas bag on the newspaper, with the handles facing toward you.

2 Pour different colors of paint onto each paper plate.

3 Use the paintbrush to paint the palm of your hand with the color of your choosing.

4 Make a ghost on your bag by pressing the palm of your hand on the canvas bag. Make sure your fingers point away from the handles.

5 Repeat using different colors. Let the paint dry.

6 Glue the wiggle eyes to each of the ghost prints.

7 Add other decorations, such as glitter, to the bag to make it more colorful.

8 When the bag is completely dry, use it to go trick-or-treating.

Celebrating Today

Today, people celebrate Halloween in many ways. Trick-or-treating is still popular with children. Costume parties are popular with both adults and children. These parties may involve Halloween-themed games, music, and food.

Homes and gardens are often decorated to look like creepy haunted mansions. Fake bats, skeletons, ghosts, tombstones, and carved pumpkins are just some of the items used to create a scary display. Many decorations are black and orange. These are the traditional colors of Halloween.

Bobbing for Apples

Bobbing for apples is a popular activity at Halloween parties.

What You Need

- large bucket or tub filled with 3/4 water
- apples

2 Easy Steps to Bob for Apples

1. Place the apples in the water so they float.

2. Have people take turns trying to pick up an apple from the bucket using only their teeth.

Jack O' Lantern

Jack o'lanterns are one of the most common **symbols** of Halloween. In the past, they were made from turnips. Today, they are made from pumpkins. People remove the pulp from inside the pumpkin and carve a face into the shell. A candle inside the pumpkin lights up the face. On Halloween, jack o'lanterns are put in windows and on front porches to greet trick-or-treaters.

Every year, more than 900 million pounds (408 million kilograms) of pumpkin are sold in the United States. Many of these pumpkins are carved and lit with a flickering candle for Halloween.

Craft a Pumpkin Candy Container

Use this candy container to keep your candy safe in one place.

What You Need

- a clean, glass jar with lid
- black paint
- green tissue paper
- ribbon
- newspaper
- glue
- paintbrush
- scissors
- orange candy

7 Easy Steps to Complete Your Candy Container

1 Spread out the newspaper.

2 Using the black paint, paint a jack o'lantern face on your jar. Allow the paint to dry.

3 Fill the jar with orange candies.

4 Cut two or three sheets of tissue paper. The pieces should be long enough to wrap around the edge of the lid and overlap slightly. The sheets need to be tall enough to twist into a pumpkin stem.

5 Brush glue onto the edge of your lid. Wrap tissue paper around it. Then, gently twist the tissue into a stem.

6 Wrap ribbon or raffia around the base of the stem.

7 When the glue is dry, attach the lid to the jar.

Black Cats

Black cats are another popular Halloween symbol. Walls and windows are often decorated with cutouts of black cats arching their backs. Black cats are often seen as spooky and mysterious creatures.

In the past, people believed that black cats had special powers and abilities. Some people thought that a black cat's actions could tell them what would happen in the future. A black cat crossing someone's path was thought to bring bad luck.

Black Cat Bookmark

You should not mind if this black cat crosses your path. He is marking your page.

What You Need

- roll or sheet of adhesive magnets
- black card stock
- white card stock
- glue
- pencil
- scissors
- small cup (optional)

5 Easy Steps to Complete Your Bookmark

1 Fold your sheet of white card stock in half. Along the edge of the fold, draw a circle. This will be your moon. You can trace around the rim of a small cup or other round item if you wish. It is important that the fold line runs through the center of the circle.

2 Use the scissors to cut out a circle.

3 On your black card stock, draw the outline of a black cat arching its back. The cat needs to be small enough to fit onto your moon. You may need to use a book or the Internet as a drawing reference for the outline of the cat.

4 Carefully cut out your black cat, and glue it onto your moon.

5 Cut two small squares from your magnets. Peel off the adhesive backing, and stick to the inside of your moon on opposite sides. You now have a black cat bookmark.

Bats

It would not be Halloween without the bat. Bats became a symbol of Halloween because they often appeared at the Celtic festival of Samhain. During the festival, huge bonfires were often lit. People gathered around them for warmth and light. Small flying insects were also attracted to these fires for the same reason. Bats eat insects, so they followed their food to the bonfire.

Pumpkin Bat

Turn a miniature pumpkin into a bat.

What You Need

- miniature ornamental pumpkin or gourd
- black acrylic paint
- craft foam, 1 sheet each of black and white
- scissors
- glue
- black tape or masking tape
- toothpicks
- paintbrush
- newspaper
- fun fur or feathers (optional)

7 Easy Steps to Complete Your Pumpkin Bat

1. Lay your newspaper on the table. Place the pumpkin, black paint, and paintbrush on top.

2. Paint your pumpkin with the black paint. Allow it to dry.

3. While the pumpkin is drying, cut your bat wings and ears out of the black craft foam. Ears should be triangular and can be as big or small as you wish. Wings should be slightly curved on the top. Cut a half circle out of the bottom of each wing.

4. Using the white foam, cut out the eyes. An easy way to make eyes is to cut a circle in half. Then, cut a smaller circle from the flat edge of each half for the pupil. You can also cut out tiny white triangles for teeth.

5. Tape toothpicks to the back of the wings and ears along the edge that will attach to the pumpkin. Toothpicks should overhang so they can be stuck into the pumpkin. If using masking tape, it can be painted black when you are finished.

6. Glue on the eyes and teeth.

7. If using fun fur or feathers, glue them on top of the pumpkin between the ears to create a fuzzy bat.

Ghost of John

Little is known about the origins of this popular Halloween song. It is believed to be a traditional American **folk song**. It may have come from Kentucky. The song is sometimes known as "The Ghost of Tom." Who John or Tom was is unknown. The song is best sung with the third line drawn out to sound like a spooky ghost.

Ghost of John

Have you seen the Ghost of John?
Long, white bones and the rest
all gone,
Oooooooh, oooooh, oooo oooooo
ooooooooooh
Wouldn't it be chilly with no
skin on?

Traditional American Song

Make Your Own Ghost

Name this ghost whatever you like.

What You Need

- cheesecloth
- scissors
- white glue
- water
- bowl
- foil scrunched into a ball
- empty drink bottle
- newspapers
- black permanent marker

7 Easy Steps to Complete Your Ghost

1 Lay the newspaper on your work surface. Set your bottle on it.

2 Cut the cheesecloth into squares large enough to drape over your bottle. Leave some extra material gathered at the base. This will create a stable base for your ghost later. You may need two or more pieces of cheesecloth depending on how you want your ghost to look.

3 Place the ball of foil on top of your drink bottle. This will create the head of your ghost.

4 Mix up two parts glue to one part water in your bowl. Place the bowl on your newspaper.

5 One at a time, dip each piece of cheesecloth into the glue mixture so that it is completely covered. Squeeze out the excess glue. Flatten out the cheesecloth, and drape each piece over your bottle. As you add each piece, you can arrange it to have a ghostlike shape.

6 Allow the ghost to dry for 24 hours. It will become solid.

7 Lift the bottle ghost off the newspaper. Draw two round eyes and a long oval mouth on the head. Your ghost is complete and ready to haunt your house as a great decoration.

Halloween Foods

Halloween celebrations feature many different foods. Some foods, such as apples, nuts, and pumpkins, are associated with Halloween because it falls at the end of **harvest** time. Apples are one of the few traditional foods eaten during Samhain that are still a part of modern Halloween celebrations. Candy apples and toffee apples are popular treats today. Apple cakes known as "fadge" were eaten during Samhain.

Candies are the most well-known Halloween foods today. Pre-wrapped candies, some in Halloween colors, are handed out to trick-or-treaters. Miniature chocolate bars and lollipops are usually in great demand. Halloween parties often feature spooky themed foods, such as cookies shaped like bats and jack o'lanterns.

Candy Apples

Try this great Halloween apple treat.

What You Need

- 8 medium-sized apples
- 8 wooden skewers or sticks
- wax paper
- 3 cups white sugar
- 1/2 cup light corn syrup
- 1 cup water
- 1/4 teaspoon cinnamon
- 1/4 teaspoon red food coloring

8 Easy Steps to Make Your Candy Apples

1 Wash and dry the apples. Remove the stems.

2 Insert a stick where the stem would be. Take care not to go all the way through the apple.

3 Put the sugar, corn syrup, and water in a medium saucepan, and heat until the sugar has completely dissolved.

4 With an adult's help, boil the syrup until it reaches 300 °Fahrenheit (149 °Celsius) on a candy thermometer. If you do not have a thermometer, drop a small amount of syrup into cold water. If small threads appear, it is ready.

5 Remove the syrup from the heat. You can stir in the cinnamon and food coloring if you are using them.

6 Dip an apple into the syrup, and swirl it gently around to coat it. Hold it above the saucepan to let the extra syrup drip off.

7 Place the apple on a piece of wax paper to cool until hardened.

8 Repeat with the remaining apples.

What Have You Learned?

1 What is the name of the Celtic festival that started Halloween?

2 What is the day after Halloween called?

3 Why did many Irish immigrate to other countries?

4 What are the traditional colors of Halloween?

5 What vegetable was first used to make jack o'lanterns?

6 How many million pounds of pumpkin are sold every year in the USA?

7 What traditional Samhain food is still eaten at Halloween?

Glossary

Celtic: anyone who speaks or spoke a Celtic language, usually from Ireland and Scotland

famine: extreme hunger and starvation

folk song: a cultural song, often from the past

harvest: when crops are ripe

symbols: images used to stand for something else

traditions: customs handed down from generation to generation

Index

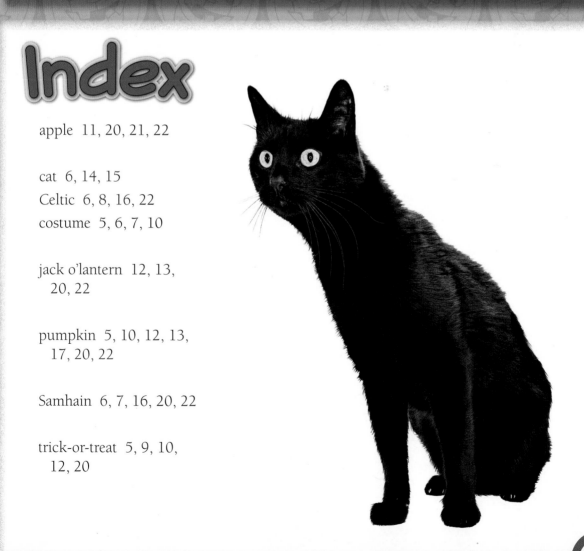

apple 11, 20, 21, 22

cat 6, 14, 15

Celtic 6, 8, 16, 22

costume 5, 6, 7, 10

jack o'lantern 12, 13, 20, 22

pumpkin 5, 10, 12, 13, 17, 20, 22

Samhain 6, 7, 16, 20, 22

trick-or-treat 5, 9, 10, 12, 20

Log on to www.av2books.com

AV² by Weigl brings you media enhanced books that support active learning. Go to www.av2books.com, and enter the special code found on page 2 of this book. You will gain access to enriched and enhanced content that supplements and complements this book. Content includes video, audio, web links, quizzes, a slide show, and activities.

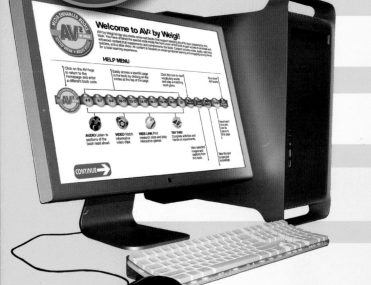

Audio
Listen to sections of the book read aloud.

Video
Watch informative video clips.

Embedded Weblinks
Gain additional information for research.

Try This!
Complete activities and hands-on experiments.

WHAT'S ONLINE?

Try This!	Embedded Weblinks	Video	EXTRA FEATURES
Try more fun activities.	Find out more about the history of Halloween.	Watch a video about Halloween.	**Audio** Listen to sections of the book read aloud.
Write a biography about an important person.	Find out more about an important holiday symbol.	Check out another video about Halloween.	**Key Words** Study vocabulary, and complete a matching word activity.
Make another recipe.	Read more information about Halloween.		**Slide Show** View images and captions, and prepare a presentation.
Play an interactive activity.	Find out about a similar celebration.		**Quizzes** Test your knowledge.

AV² was built to bridge the gap between print and digital. We encourage you to tell us what you like and what you want to see in the future.
Sign up to be an AV² Ambassador at www.av2books.com/ambassador.

Due to the dynamic nature of the Internet, some of the URLs and activities provided as part of AV² by Weigl may have changed or ceased to exist. AV² by Weigl accepts no responsibility for any such changes. All media enhanced books are regularly monitored to update addresses and sites in a timely manner. Contact AV² by Weigl at 1-866-649-3445 or av2books@weigl.com with any questions, comments, or feedback.